ABIDING IN THE PLACE OF WORSHIP

PRACTICAL INSTRUCTIONS
FOR THE
MODERN-DAY MINSTREL

ABIDING IN THE PLACE OF WORSHIP

PRACTICAL INSTRUCTIONS FOR THE MODERN-DAY MINSTREL

DR. EARNEST PUGH

Foreword By Dr. Ralph Douglas West

ABIDING IN THE PLACE OF WORSHIP

PRACTICAL INSTRUCTIONS
FOR THE MODERN-DAY MINSTREL

Published by books2liveby.com

ISBN: 978-0-9824195-2-6

Contact:

BOOKS2LIVEBY.com
700 Suttles Dr.
Atlanta, GA 30331
info@books2liveby.com

EARNEST PUGH WORLDWIDE
9659 N. Sam Houston Parkway E.
#227
Humble, Texas 77396
EarnestPugh.com

ENDORSEMENTS

Much can be concluded about people when you know where they hang out. You can often rightly judge their associations, their tastes, their habits and yes, maybe even their character based on their investment of time and geography.

Rev. Earnest Pugh rightly and Biblically reminds us that 'abiding' is qualitatively different than 'visiting'. And he teaches us what to do, while we are there. The place of WORSHIP is more than a sporadic exercise, or a copied activity. It is the anvil upon which God reveals *us* to *ourselves*, hones us into God's own image, and perfects our mutual love. Thank you sir, for putting onto paper what we have witnessed in your life and in your song throughout the years. Bravo!

Claudette Anderson Copeland, D.Min.
Pastor Emeritus, New Creation Christian Fellowship
San Antonio, Texas

Every generation has what I call its "Acts 17:6'ers." Acts 17:6 reads in part, "These who have turned the world upside down have come here too."

Dr. Earnest Pugh, whom I affectionately refer to as "The Maestro," is an Acts 17:6'er. He is not just an accomplished gospel music artist or minister of the gospel, but the core of his nature is to be a worshipper. Both his music and revelation of worship help every believer to ascend to a place of abiding in a place of worship that alters every aspect of life.

Whatever we behold, we become; and worship does for believers what knowledge alone cannot. I am certain that this book, written from his unique perspective, will spawn a transcendent experience in your worship and relationship with God.

Bishop Kevin Foreman
Pastor, Harvest Church
Denver, CO & Atlanta, GA

Earnest Pugh is known as one of God's most gifted and anointed psalmists. When he sings it is as if he's touching the very heart of God.

In this book, you will not only witness the intimate relationship Earnest has with the Holy Spirit as a gospel singer and psalmist, but you will also experience a gifted and anointed theologian and Minister of the Gospel of Jesus Christ.

I have been blessed to see him mature in music and in ministry now for the last twenty-five years. This book offers insight and wisdom from a seasoned man of faith whose life experiences have uniquely equipped him to be a vessel through which the Holy Spirit flows.

Abiding in the Place of Worship will inspire you, inform you, educate you, but most of all help propel you forward to the place in God's kingdom that God has for you.

If you have been inspired by Earnest Pugh's singing, get ready to go to another level, as he writes with the same anointing he sings with. This book will help you go to a deeper place as you abide in your own place of worship and fellowship with God.

Rev. Dr. Grainger Browning Jr.
Senior Pastor, Ebenezer AME Church
Fort Washington, MD

Many know Earnest Pugh as the stellar musician with an outstanding ability to lead others into worship. Yet I'm grateful, having been personally connected to him and his ministry for well over two decades, to know him as a highly skilled and equipped biblical scholar with both a Master of Divinity and Doctor of Ministry degree from the prestigious Howard University School of Divinity. Not only is Dr. Pugh academically astute, he is an anointed prophetic teacher and preacher.

Through Dr. Pugh's book, you will be able to take the journey that leads to worship as your dwelling place. You will be transformed from thinking of worship as a place of visitation to thinking of it as a place of habitation.

Earnest has masterfully crafted this book to encourage readers to embrace worship as a sacred abiding place where moment-by-moment communion in the presence of a loving God takes place. Dr. Pugh walks you through scripture, bringing revelation about the beautiful place we live, called worship.

As you take this amazing journey, prepare to be enriched as you go from visitation to habitation. I salute you, Earnest, my brother and friend for your labor of love and wisdom shared in *Abiding in the Place of Worship*.

Steven W. Banks, M.Div.
Apostle, Life Coach
Author of *Healing the Father Wound*

There is no weapon in the saints' arsenal like the weapon of worship. Worship is not only a right and responsibility, it is the way we reward God for who He is, and it is the place where God meets us.

In this dynamic book, *Abiding in the Place of Worship,* Dr. Pugh helps us activate a new hunger for perpetually hosting the Lord's presence.

Through sound interpretation of scripture, situational life illustrations, and decisive calls to action, Dr. Pugh takes us into an uncommon depth of revelation knowledge about the believer's call to worship. He also reveals the power, benefits, and capacity of God's presence to bless, heal, strengthen, correct, and yes, even prosper us.

Dr. Pugh tackles the often overlooked hindrances to worship, such as the attitude of our hearts, the spirit of reproach, the danger of unconfessed sin, and so much more. This book will make you a better and more committed worshipper.

Victor S. Couzens, D.Min.
Lead Pastor, Inspirational Bible Church
Cincinnati, OH

Dr. Earnest Pugh, one of the most prolific gospel singers of our time, shares with us how critical true worship is in the life of a believer, particularly during this season of uncertainty as our nation is threatened by the spread of the COVID-19 pandemic and racial unrest.

Abiding in the Place of Worship helps us find our own essential authentic, personal, and intimate relationship with God.

Real worship must first and foremost happen in the heart of the child of God. This connection helps us to understand that we can worship our God at any time and in any place. This intimate place of worship assists us during seasons of attack when we need the explosive power of God to sustain us and give us victory.

Our position of abiding in Christ is at the core of genuine worship and helps us avoid the distractions of our carnal nature.

Through this book worship leaders will gain insight and elevate their thinking about the true nature of the authentic place of worship, which is the heart.

Michael E. Bell Sr.
Senior Pastor, Allen Chapel AME Church
Washington, DC

Dear Reader,

It is my great honor to present this book to you! However, I want you to be doubly blessed by the addition of the companion musical CD that I have prepared esspecially to compliment this book. I know it will encourage you as you read. To purchase the CD visit: EarnestPugh.com

CONTENTS

Section Three
LOVE BUILDS OTHERS UP

ACKNOWLEDGEMENTS

I believe this book is going to be transformative to multiple thousands of believers! It is the result of thoughts and ideas that began more than thirty years ago through various praise and worship seminars, workshops, and one-on-one impartations regarding how worshippers and worship leaders can direct the flow of worship—privately and publicly.

You will note that I preface every point with the fact that it's not enough to merely visit the place of worship; real transformation only occurs as a result of living, dwelling, and abiding in the place of worship.

Gratitude compels me to acknowledge the many people who have been part of this rich journey. Their influence and input could never be reflected on sheets of paper. The hundreds of hours of dialogue, prayer, training, and teaching have enriched my life beyond the expression that words can offer. In large part, they are part of this book, and my name should not stand alone on this title page.

My deepest appreciation to the Late Apostle Nathaniel Holcomb, who began pushing me into my purpose (as a worshipper) when I was just twenty years old and has continued to speak into my life.

Secondly, I salute the faculty and staff of Howard University School of Divinity, where my life was forever changed while under the tutelage of some of the country's most prolific professors, preachers, and teachers.

Several people deserve special mention for sharing their ministry platforms and counsel over the years: Bishop Darryl S. Brister, Elder Byron Cage, Apostle Steven Banks, Bishop Victor Couzens, Pastor Terry (Renee) Hornbuckle, and Rev. Dr. Grainger Browning, who pulled on my worship mantle for several years during his midweek Bible Studies and who pronounced a "Prophetic Benediction" over me in 2009 (during my "Rain On Us" recording) that changed the trajectory of my ministry as a psalmist. To Pastor Michael Bell (Allen Chapel AME Church) for platforming me in the presence of former President Barack Obama and his family (Michelle, Sasha and Malia) on Easter 2010 which catapulted my life, ministry, and career on the majestic heights of success. Thank you!

Of course, none of this would be possible without my mom, the late Lillie Pearl Pugh, who prophesied this book into existence in December 2006 while on her deathbed.

My deepest thanks to Dr.Teresa Hairston, who possesses the unique ability to eloquently draw out my heart's sentiments, causing the deep to call upon the deep! What a gift to the world you are!

Finally, to my village: My daughter Kira, Keith Williams, Zaunder Saucer,Troy Clark, Jentrega Hayes, Vanzil Burke and Burke Management Team; and my amazing animals: Muffin, Blackie, and Zeus.

Earnestly Yours,
Earnest Pugh Worldwide

PREFACE

Have you ever encountered a person who seemingly is under perpetual attack from the enemy? Perhaps the attack is directed at that person's health, finances, job, or career. It could be that their family members are at odds. In that person's life, it's as if the enemy is relentlessly attacking every area. However, if you look closer, you can trace the chaos back, at some point or other, to the fact that this person has left his or her "place" or position of worship and is no longer in a close relationship with God.

To be in a close relationship with God means to abide or dwell in God's presence. According to SermonIndex.net, the word "abide" is translated from the Greek word *meno*. It means "to remain in the same place or position over a period of time. To reside, stay, live, lodge, tarry or dwell." Meno describes something that remains where it is, continues in a fixed state, or endures.

As believers, the status of *abiding* in Christ refers to the maintenance of an intimate relationship with Him (see John 6:56; I John 2:24, 28; 3:6). Worshippers can choose to abide in Christ or abide in darkness. If we abide in Christ, we dwell in a place of safety. However, outside of Christ, we expose ourselves to the plans and devices of the enemy.

When we refer to the "place" of worship, we are not describing a physical building. Many times, because of our Christian tradition of going to a building to fellowship with others, we say we are "going" to worship. The heart of the true worshipper hungers and thirsts for the presence of God.

Actually, the primary "place" of worship is the heart. God desires that the hearts of His children "follow hard after Him" (Ps. 63:8) and commune with Him.

Conversely, the heart of the carnal-minded person who may even consider himself a worshipper is often more concerned with culture, tradition, and ritual, rather than relationship. A carnal worshipper doesn't seek transformation nor does he or she earnestly desire the manifestation of the glory of God. This person has been distracted by the enemy and has either left the place of worship or never truly been there.

In this critical season, it's imperative that we understand that we are at war and the enemy of our souls wants to distract us so that he can destroy us! In

John 10, Jesus contrasts himself with the thief: *"The thief does not come except to steal, and to kill, and to destroy. I have come that they may have life, and that they may have it more abundantly"* (John 10:10). Paul makes it clear that in order to "abide" in God's presence, which is the place of abundance and safety, we must have knowledge of the enemy's tactics, *"lest Satan should take advantage of us; for we are not ignorant of his devices"* (2 Cor. 2:11).

In this book, my goals are as follows:

- To expose many of the devices that have been used by the enemy to distract and derail us from the place (presence) of God.

- To encourage the heart of worshippers and worship leaders. More than ever, worshippers must understand their roles and responsibilities. For those who stand before people and lead them in worship, you must first be in your place of worship. This is imperative.

- To elevate your thinking as it relates to your influence as a leader. When God positions you in a place of oversight, He also endows you with insight. This only comes from spending time in God's presence. Sight is important. When you are a leader, you must see farther than those you lead in order to guide, protect, and direct them.

My prayer is that this book will open your eyes to the opportunities that God has placed in your hands to impact the world!

Sincerely,

Earnest L. Pugh, M.Div., D.Min.

FOREWORD

In John 4, Jesus responded to the woman at the well that God was looking for true worshippers. They, who come to God, must worship Him in spirit and in truth.

True worshippers are those who do not focus on fixed locations, certain times, or pristine conditions. The true worshipper worships God constantly. His or her life is committed to an existence that adores the living God. But we need to be reminded of this truth, do we not?

We need to be reminded that life and its endless changes and turns will throw obstacles in our way that will inhibit the free flow of worship to the Lord, our God.

For this reason, I am thankful for this wonderful book that reminds us of the essentiality of living a life filled with worship. Earnest Pugh brings attention to worship as a corporate activity, in song and service, and as an individual obligation for the believer.

When you read this book, you will be awakened to the transformative power that is available when you commit yourself to a worshipful life. You will be compelled to stay in the place of worship, and there you will discover God's empowering presence.

Dr. Ralph Douglas West
Senior Pastor, Church Without Walls
Houston, TX

INTRODUCTION

The "Love" Issue

"The Parable of the Good Samaritan" is found in Luke 10:25–37. It begins with a man who is described as "an expert in the law" (v. 25) posing a question to Jesus. This question is one that every believer wants the answer to: "What must I do to inherit eternal life?"

This man knew the Torah, so he wasn't some neophyte looking to learn; he was actually testing Jesus's knowledge. He was probably a mature, older man, acknowledged in his day as a religious scholar, who looked at the youthfulness of Jesus and thought, "What does he really know?"

When Jesus answered the man, He didn't give a briefing on the 613 commandments of the Torah. No! Jesus brilliantly pointed to the one most powerful concept in the entire body of Scripture, the concept of "love."

"And He answering said,Thou shalt love the Lord thy God with all thy heart, and with all thy soul, and with all thy strength, and with all thy mind; and thy neighbour as thyself" (Luke 10:27, KJV).

Jesus's simple yet profound response summarized the 613 commandments into two: every believer who desires eternal life must first love God and then love others.

I John 4:16 confirms, "God is love; and he that dwelleth in love dwelleth in God, and God in him." To "dwell" or abide in the place of worship means that your heart must abide in the place of agape, which is "a pure, willful, sacrificial love that intentionally desires another's highest good" (Christianity.com). The core of worship is agape. It's important to understand that our worship comes from a heart response to God because He first loved us. Therefore, worship is an agape response that is initiated, directed, and led by God.

Throughout his ministry, Jesus used parables as a simple way to communicate complex themes. The parable of the Good Samaritan has been told multiple times and interpreted by millions of believers. However, in this book, we will examine its meaning in its application to the twenty-first century worshipper and worship leader.

In Luke 10:25–37, we find the full text of "The Parable of the Good Samaritan":

"And behold, a certain lawyer stood up and tested Him, saying, "Teacher, what shall I do to inherit eternal life?"

He said to him, "What is written in the law? What is your reading of it?"

So, he answered and said, "You shall love the Lord your God with all your heart, with all your soul, with all your strength, and with all your mind, and your neighbor as yourself."

And He said to him, "You have answered rightly; do this and you will live."

But he, wanting to justify himself, said to Jesus, "And who is my neighbor?"

Then Jesus answered and said: "A certain man went down from Jerusalem to Jericho, and fell among thieves, who stripped him of his clothing, wounded him, and departed, leaving him half dead. Now by chance a certain priest came down that road. And when he saw him, he passed by on the other side. Likewise a Levite, when he arrived at the place, came and looked, and passed by on the other side. But a certain Samaritan, as he journeyed, came where he was. And when he saw him, he had compassion. So he went to him and bandaged his wounds, pouring on oil and wine; and he set him on his own animal, brought him to an inn, and took care of him. On the next day, when he departed, he took out two denarii, gave them to the innkeeper, and said to him, 'Take care of him; and whatever more you spend, when I come again, I will repay you.' So which of these three do you think was a neighbor to him who fell among the thieves?"

And he said, "He who showed mercy on him."

Then Jesus said to him, "Go and do likewise."

In this passage, Jesus echoes the Levitical command found in Lev. 19:18, *"You shall not take vengeance or bear a grudge against any of your people, but you shall love your neighbor as yourself: I am the Lord."* The idea of loving your neighbor as yourself does not mean love someone like you love yourself. It is better translated, love (agape) those who are part of your community and are similar to you.

However, the commands don't just consider those who are similar; they also consider those who are not part of your community. In Lev. 19:34, we read: *"The stranger who dwells among you shall be to you as one born among you, and you shall love him as yourself; for you were strangers in the land of Egypt: I am the Lord your God."* This verse commands, not suggests, that you show love to those who are different from you, whether that difference is denominational, racial, socioeconomic, or philosophical. The inference is that you should love others, no matter how different from you, as unconditionally as God loves you.

In today's society and culture, much has been made about the differences among classes, races, and philosophies. In fact, we often spend more time dwelling on differences rather than similarities. The truth is, we are all precious in the sight of God, and He is pleased when we minimize division and embrace unity. Our Heavenly Father is pleased when His children love each other and realize that we are the sheep of one pasture.

Love is the Foundation of Worship

We are commanded to love others as ourselves. Love is not a noun, it's a verb, an action word. Jesus instructed, "If you love me, keep my commandments" (John 14:15).

When I was on active duty as a Corporal in the United States Army, I was given oversight of a platoon. It was my first time in such a position. My troops were often required to rise early in the morning to complete various tasks. Sometimes they had to also work on weekends.

I was young, and many times my troops weren't always respectful of my position. One day, I remembered my supervisor telling me, "You're a Noncommissioned
Officer! You're not on the same level as the troops.

When they have to get up early, stay up late, or work on weekends, you can assign your Squad Leader to oversee them; you don't have to be there."

I understood what he was saying. However, I never missed an opportunity to share in the "extra" duties. The reason was, I wanted to let them know that we were in it together. I wanted them to know that I was pulling for them. As time went on, when some of the troops needed to do extra exercises, I would join them. I'd be right there sweating with them.

It wasn't easy. At first, several of them gave me a hard time, but eventually it became easier because they saw me make sacrifices to let them know that my rank didn't mean that I didn't care about them. Eventually, I won them over with my actions. My point is, actions speak louder than words!

Loving Your Neighbor Requires Taking Initiative

It is only when we come to a true understanding of love in action that we can understand how to love others.

Often, the best way a person can exhibit his or her love for God is in how they love other people. It doesn't matter how gifted and talented you are, or how much money or status you have. If you can't demonstrate your love to others, you aren't really abiding in the place of worship.

SECTION ONE

The Importance of Abiding

Chapter One

WORSHIPPERS! DON'T LEAVE THE "HIGH PLACE!"

Then Jesus answered and said: "A certain man went down from Jerusalem to Jericho, and fell among thieves." *(Luke 10:30)*

Let's consider the setting of this text. The elevation of Jerusalem is 2,592 feet above sea level. It is literally is the "high place," whereas Jericho is 846 feet below sea level. The climate conditions between the cities were also very different. Jerusalem was more of a Mediterranean climate (warm, dry summers and cool, mild winters) and Jericho was hot and tropical. In fact, Jericho was (and remains) an oasis situated in the midst of a desert. Although the distance between the two cities is less than twenty miles, in Jesus's day the route was dangerous and difficult. It was known as the Way of Blood because of the blood that was often shed there by robbers.

Jesus uses this well-known route as the setting for this parable, but we can also see this as an illustration of how leaving the high place (the place of worship) can expose you to danger.

Once you have experienced the glory of God (the high place) and you depart from it, or cease to "abide" there, you spiral downward and find yourself in a state of vulnerability.

In the parable, Jesus does not indicate why the man left Jerusalem. There could have been any number of reasons. In Jesus's day, certainly the road to Jericho was dangerous, but because of Jericho's geographical positioning and tropical climate, it was an oasis in the desert. Jericho was an important center of agriculture and commerce. Perhaps the man was going to Jericho to do business or to vacation. Jesus doesn't indicate the man's reason, but perhaps that's intentional!

Is there ever a good reason for leaving the high place? Why does anyone leave their place of worship? Let's consider the situations that may cause you to depart from abiding in the presence of God.

Tribulations

Tribulations, which can be characterized as "three times the trouble," can convince you to leave the high place.

Tribulations can include internal and external pressure, which is any form of distress, anguish, and affliction.The Bible teaches us that in this life we will all experience tribulations. In John 16:33, we read, *"These things I have spoken to you, that in Me you may have peace. In the world you will have tribulation; but be of good cheer, I have overcome the world."*

The enemy sends tribulations in the form of attacks on your spirit, body, and mind, with the intent of derailing your future. Remaining connected to the word of God is the key to overcoming tribulations.

It's not what you go through in life, it's how you go through it.

Be sure to "grow" through what you "go" through. The objective is to grow! Sometimes, we have the wrong perspective of tribulations.

God often uses tribulations to grow us, so the question you must ask yourself is, "Am I growing through this, or just going through this?"

Training is a huge part of Army life. One day, my Drill Sergeant announced, "We're going to do resistance training." We had already been working out with push-ups and other exercises, but now, through this resistance training, we would be able to build more core and muscular strength. The goal of resistance training is to improve muscle strength and endurance. This is also accomplished through strength training or weight lifting. During a resistance-training workout, you move your limbs against resistance provided by your body weight, gravity, bands, weighted bars, or dumbbells.

Tribulations are like spiritual resistance training. They build your faith muscles. You are able to endure more because of tribulations. James wrote, "knowing that the testing of your faith produces patience. But let patience have its perfect work, that you may be perfect and complete, lacking nothing" (James 1:3–4).

Sometimes we have the wrong perspective of tribulations. We look at them as challenges to avoid or as a reason to quit, but God uses tribulation to help intensify your worship.

Distractions

Distractions are another area of attack. Distractions can cause broken fellowship. When the enemy lures you out of God's presence he starts with a toehold, which leads to a foothold, and then leads to a stronghold.

Toehold. Foothold. Stronghold.

A "toehold" is disrupted fellowship. When there is a disruption in your service to God, the enemy gets a "toehold." Perhaps you used to serve in a local auxiliary at your church, but you quit or took an *indefinite* break. You might have been part of the choir or the praise team or even in the band. When you don't do your part, you don't feel a part, and the enemy can use that disruption in your fellowship to alienate you. That's the toehold.

Then there is the foothold, which is a total breakdown in your fellowship with God. This can happen when you stop attending church altogether. You stop paying tithes and no longer have an interest in watching your church's services online or streaming. Perhaps you begin to look at movies or start fellowshipping with others who are not believers.

This leads to a stronghold. At this point, you have no desire for fellowship with God. You no longer have a hunger or thirst for His presence or fellowship with His people, as you once did. At this point, you are most vulnerable to the enemy's distractions.

In order to avoid this trap, you must *"Keep your heart with all diligence, For out of it spring the issues of life"* (Prov. 4:23). As long as you are in fellowship with God's presence and His people, you are able to stand strong against these *holds* in your life.

Church Hurt

Being hurt in the place that is supposed to be the house of healing can be devastating. Church hurt comes as a result of something said or done by another believer that causes your soul to be wounded. Maybe it was betrayal or mistreatment,or perhaps you were criticized unfairly, dismissed from a position, or blamed for something you didn't do. The list goes on.

The question you must ask is, "Am I going to allow this hurt to elevate me or devastate me?"

Wounds from church hurt can form scabs that continue to be reopened. Wounds cause vulnerability and lead to *cycles of pain*. In other words, hurting people hurt other people. To avoid being a wounded worshipper and to break the cycle of pain is to return to the high place.

Solomon wrote about the security of the high place. "The name of the Lord is a strong tower; The righteous run to it and are safe" (Prov. 18:10). God's name conveys His character. He is a refuge. David reassures us in Ps. 91:1–4, "He who dwells in the secret place of the Most High shall abide under the shadow of the Almighty. I will say of the Lord, 'He is my refuge and my fortress; My God, in Him I will trust.' Surely He shall deliver you from the snare of the fowler and from the perilous pestilence. He shall cover you with His feathers, and under His wings you shall take refuge; His truth shall be your shield and buckler."

When you are reeling from emotional pain, instead of running away from God, run to Him! That's the safe place. The Bible confirms this again in James 4:8, *"Draw near to God and He will draw near to you."* When you are in the high place (the presence of God), He will shield you from everything that's contrary to His will, word, and way!

You might have experienced hurt and devastation many times, but God's word confirms that when you call Him, He hears you. He inclines His ear toward you. When someone reclines, they lie back. This is the opposite of inclining. When God's children cry out to Him through praise, prayer, and worship, He sits up to hear them.

Let the Wound Heal!

Another important consideration is whether or not you are allowing the wound to heal. If you want it to heal, you must stop touching it! Every time you have a conversation about the words or actions that caused the wound, you keep it from healing. Each time you rehearse thoughts about the wound, you prevent it from healing.

The remedy for your wound is prayer, praise, and worship that connects your spirit with the Holy Spirit. Praise magnifies God above your internal and external conflicts. David declared, "But You *are* holy, Enthroned in the praises of Israel" (Ps. 22:3).

Prayer brings you into intimacy with God, and you begin to see others as God sees them.

Paul writes, *"And we know that all things work together for good to those who love God, to those who are the called according to His purpose"* (Rom. 8:28). We often hear people say, "Prayer changes things," but when you pray for God's will to be done, regardless of what has happened to you, He will literally turn situations and perspectives around and make it happen for you!

Worship heals the wound because it stabilizes your spirit, brings you into unity with God, and allows healing to take place.

If you need healing, you need to get hungry! Because when you hunger and thirst and seek after God, He will respond and fill you with His Spirit! God promises, "*Blessed are those who hunger and thirst for righteousness, For they shall be filled*" (Matt. 5:6).

Magnify God above Everything

When you magnify God above your situations and circumstances, you make Him bigger, and that perspective allows healing to take place. However, the converse is also true. When you magnify your situations and circumstances, you are essentially saying that the situation is bigger than God and this prevents the healing process.

It's important that you realize the power of your praise, prayer, and worship can usher you back into the high place. When you are in God's presence, things like tribulations, distractions, and church hurt cannot overwhelm you. His presence enables you to forgive, release, face, trace, and erase! Paul reminds us, "Now the Lord is the Spirit; and where the Spirit of the Lord *is*, there *is* liberty" (2 Cor. 3:17).

As you meditate on this chapter, please listen to:

"FREE TO WORSHIP"

Chapter Two

WHAT HAPPENS "ALONG THE WAY"

Then Jesus answered and said: "A certain man went down from Jerusalem to Jericho, and fell among thieves, who stripped him of his clothing, wounded him, and departed, leaving him half dead." (Luke 10:30)

We've already discussed the fact that leaving the high place exposes you to perpetual attacks of the enemy. Satan's specialty is finding your areas of vulnerability and pounding those areas.

The fact that bandits robbed, beat, stripped, and abandoned the man speaks to the fact that this man was physically, emotionally, and spiritually brutalized. He was lying there on the side of the road.

Although this man might have voluntarily left the high place, he probably never intended to end up in such a terrible predicament. This half-dead situation is very important for us to acknowledge.

There are people who are functioning in ministry that are half-dead. They've been through so much and have been wounded so severely that they are really not fulfilling the call of God with joy and gladness. They are barely alive.

This is a serious situation, and it is all very prevalent in today's churches. I can testify that the weight of ministry can be so severe that you can find yourself in a very dysfunctional place.

In my situation, I had been doing all that I could to be attentive to my duties at church, while at the same time trying to advance my career. I was stretching myself and trying to please everyone around me. I was going from services to concerts and doing all the things that made it look like I was being productive. Meanwhile, I was dying inside because I wasn't spending enough time in the presence of God (what I call the Throne Room).

In order to grow in God, you must spend time with Him.

I believe that spending time in the word of God each day is imperative. David declared, *"The entrance of Your words gives light; it gives understanding to the simple"* (Ps. 119:130). This scripture underscores the fact that the light of God's Holy Spirit illuminates your pathway; conversely, where there is an absence of light, which is darkness, you will stumble and fall.

When you study the word of God daily, you get more and more revelation, and you become more like Jesus. The telltale sign that a person has become spiritually stagnant is that they begin to say the same things over and over. What's in your heart abundantly, comes out of your mouth eventually. Jesus said, *"For out of the abundance of the heart the mouth speaks"* (Matt. 12:34).

Half-Dead Worshippers Are not Creative

Half-dead worshippers function in tradition and make comments like, "This is the way we've always done it" or "This is good enough." They make no effort to innovate because they are half-dead! If you are a psalmist or worship leader, you ought to speak fresh words and phrases as you minister.

Beware of saying the same things over and over; this is a sign that you are not growing in the word of God. Take time to rehearse the word of God. Rehearse God's word more than your music! Make sure you understand the scriptural basis for the songs that you sing. Don't be lax in studying the scriptures that are the foundation for the words of the songs that you sing. Find out the meaning of the Scripture by studying the original language.

You should always *pray it before you praise it!* This means pray your songs before you lift your songs in praise. In order for you to effectively *lead* people somewhere, you must first go there yourself!

Half-dead believers are unloving; they treat others with contempt rather than concern. They rehearse how they have been mistreated and make others feel inferior, as though they ought to be glad to be favored with their presence! Oh, yes, they don't mind saying all the right things, but when it comes to putting love in action, they don't extend themselves because they're half dead.

Half-dead believers are stagnant in their growth. They go through the motions of prayer and make a pretense of praise and worship. They use their gifts and talents in an outward show but don't open their heart to allow God's word to penetrate. They are often critical of the church and its leadership. They may tithe, but they don't give much else because they're half dead.

In the book of James, we learn, *"For as the body without the spirit is dead, so faith without works is dead also"* (2:26). James affirms that deeds (or actions) are the by-product of a living faith. Works do not justify us or make us righteous before God nor are they the means to salvation. Rather, our deeds are the fruit that is produced from someone who has been transformed by God's grace and is living in obedience to God's commands.

Are you "half dead?" I can relate because I've been there.

As a Worship Pastor or Praise Leader going from one assignment to another, I picked up some severe scars along the way. I stayed in some positions much longer than I should have because I reasoned, "This is my vocation!" Even though I knew that the anointing had lifted for that particular assignment, and I no longer had the grace to run that specific race, I remained in the position. I was in great danger and didn't even know it.

> *At one particular assignment, I was literally running the clock out like a basketball player. The money was good, and I had become quite comfortable, but honestly, I was leading while bleeding. I was half dead.*

The Danger of being half dead and maintaining your leadership position is that you often move from one place to another with gaping wounds that no one can see. As a result, you bleed on people who didn't cut you.

Furthermore, because of the infection inside, you are no longer as effective. I moved from one place to another, but I was half dead.

As we will discuss later, anyone who is leading but is half dead will never be able to rise to their maximum effectiveness unless until they come to grips with their situation and address their wound(s).

Addressing Your Wounds

For the sake of clarity, addressing your situation does not mean confronting your leader. The first step is self-care. The first medication you need is prayer. Take your concerns to God and Him alone. Discussing your wounds with friends, co-laborers, and loved ones only keeps the wounds open and prohibits healing. Every time you open up that conversation you give the wounds life and relevancy.

Medical research indicates that a complexity of factors impact the healing of wounds. Simply put, first, you must stop the bleeding. Second, the wound must be exposed to the right balance of oxygen. Too much or too little oxygen delays the healing process. It is also important in this stage for the wound not to become infected by unhealthy bacteria. In other words, you have to keep the wound area clean. Third, there is a rebuilding process where a scar develops and new tissue forms. Finally, strength returns to the area where the wounds originally occurred. It might take months or even years for this process, depending on the severity of the original wounds.

Open wounds that never heal can be fatal. As you consider Jesus's parable and this man who was wounded, consider your own status. Are you walking around half dead and attempting to function with open wounds that have become infected?

Sources of spiritual infection can include your close friends and associates; an unhealthy work environment or relationship at your local church; or your own thoughts that continue to replay the scenes of the incidents that caused the wounds.

It's time to face it, trace it, and erase it.

LET'S PRAY!

Dear Lord, I come to you as a worshipper who loves You with my whole heart, mind, and soul. I commit my life to You, not just with lip service but with the totality of my thoughts, words, and actions.

I acknowledge that the foundation of my worship is built on the fact that You first loved me. I realize that my love response to You can only be seen by others when I express it through the things I do and the love (agape) I show toward others.

I commit to guard my heart with all diligence because I know that out of it flows the issues of life. I commit to resist temptation and not to allow prejudice or hatred to exist in my heart.

I pray against division, alienation, negativity, malice, gossip, and bigotry. I continually cleanse my heart of thoughts that don't align with Your word. My desire is to abide in Your presence and worship You with a pure heart so that You may receive my worship as a sweet-smelling savor to Your nostrils.

In Jesus's Name, Amen.

SECTION TWO

Love in Action

Chapter Three

WORSHIPPERS MUST ADDRESS NEEDS

Now by chance a certain priest came down that road. And when he saw him, he passed by on the other side. Likewise a Levite, when he arrived at the place, came and looked, and passed by on the other side. (Luke 10:31–32)

It is difficult to understand why a priest and a Levite would see this man lying on the roadside in obvious need of emergency assistance and not stop to help. But let's be honest and ask ourselves: In the context of our busy lives, how many of us are similarly guilty?

I want to stretch you a bit here. In the first section of this book, I asked you to look at this parable from the perspective of the man who left the high place and was attacked and left half-dead. But now I want you to look from the perspective of the Samaritan, because that's really where Jesus wanted our focus to be. We will see that more clearly later.

Why did the priest pass the man by? Perhaps he was coming from Jerusalem and had been serving in the temple. Maybe he was afraid of touching the wounded man for fear that the man's blood would make him ceremonially unclean.

What about the Levite? A Levite was assigned the role of singing and serving in the temple. Levites performed a variety of tasks, from maintenance to teaching. The Levite was accustomed to serving, but here he walks by on the other side of the road.

We know that both men saw the need, but we also know that both did not respond to the need. Likewise, our challenge today is what to do when we see a need.

Whether we are in the church, at home, or at work, there are often people that we see in various states of need, but we don't respond!

How many people have you encountered who needed a kind word, a token of love, or a friendly gesture? How many people, especially these days, are you willing to assist with food, shelter, clothing, or other resources?

The Bible shows us many examples of Jesus's concern for the physical needs of people. He wasn't so spiritually minded that He was no earthly good. He fed the hungry and healed the sick.

My mother used to tell me, "*You* become so that *others* can become!" Real ministry is about "we" not "me." When we look at the establishment of the church in the book of Acts, we find that it was based on a community (common unity), where believers shared everything. If one lacked something, the others gave of their substance. We know that *"The earth is the Lord's, and all its fullness, the world and those who dwell therein"* (Ps. 24:1). Everything we have is because God allowed us to have it. Being selfish is ungodly. We are blessed to be a blessing.

As a part of the music industry, I often hear artists talk about the business aspect of gospel music. And while I understand that this is a business and that it is a means of income, I also understand that God is my ultimate supplier, and regardless of whether I'm paid or not, He deserves my worship. *My gift is mine to steward.* That means that I handle it as though it actually belongs to Him, not me.

When you think about your resources, your time, talent, and treasure (money), do you handle these items as though they are *on loan* from God? If you see a need, do you quickly step in to offer your time, talent, and treasure? Or, do you act in the same manner as the priest and the Levite?

Too many believers are passing by "on the other side." We avoid the calls from people who we don't believe have resources to compensate us. We dodge people at events who have been trying to get our help. The problem is, God is watching you and He desires for you to respond! The response you give now is critical to your promotion because you're showing God that you can *stand* to be blessed.

I believe that during the season of COVID-19 and racial unrest, and especially beyond, it is critical that believers across the world rise up and respond. We must open our mouths, lift our voices, and take action to *be* the church instead of being stuck in the tradition of just *having* church!

God spoke to His people several times in the scripture about helping others. This is what He calls "true religion" (James 1:27). Isaiah 58:10 says, "If you extend your soul to the hungry and satisfy the afflicted soul, then your light shall dawn in the darkness and your darkness shall be as the noonday."

In the Gospel of Luke, we find that John the Baptist rebuked "religious" people in favor of those who needed help: "Then he said to the multitudes that came out to be baptized by him, 'Brood of vipers! Who warned you to flee from the wrath to come? Therefore bear fruits worthy of repentance, and do not begin to say to yourselves, 'We have Abraham as our father.' For I say to you that God is able to raise up children to Abraham from these stones. And even now the ax is laid to the root of the trees. Therefore every tree which does not bear good fruit is cut down and thrown into the fire.' So the people asked him, saying, 'What shall we do then?' He answered and said to them, 'He who has two tunics, let him give to him who has none; and he who has food, let him do likewise'" (Luke 3:7–11).

The early church gave food to people and made sure that widows were taken care of (Acts 6:1; 1Tim. 5).

As you consider your church, community, and city, what opportunities are available for you to serve? This is a good time to reposition your resources so that you can resist passing by "on the other side."

As you meditate on this chapter, please listen to:

"MORE OF YOU"

Chapter Four

WORSHIPPERS MUST EXTEND KINDNESS TO ALL "NATIONS"

Now by chance a certain priest came down that road. And when he saw him, he passed by on the other side. Likewise a Levite, when he arrived at the place, came and looked, and passed by on the other side. (Luke 10:31–32)

Jesus lets us know specifics about the races and creeds of the men who appear in this Good Samaritan parable. The priest and Levite are Jewish, and they are devout, meaning they are honored to serve in the temple in Jerusalem. The man lying on the road half dead was probably Jewish as well; however, he was likely not of the same class or distinction as the religious men. Perhaps he was just a common person from an everyday, run-of-the-mill background.

Since the dawn of time, human beings have struggled to embrace and appreciate those who are different in their appearance, beliefs, and practices. The culprit that encourages someone to think himself better than another is pride. One theologian stated that people often erroneously exhibit pride in three areas: *race, grace (faith), and face.*

Avoid Racial Pride

Racial pride, which assigns ideologies of inferiority, superiority, or prejudice based on the color of a person's skin, has led to catastrophic outcomes. African Americans are all too familiar with the horrors of the slave trade, which saw millions of Africans uprooted from their homes and villages and brought to the shores of America to be traded and treated as commodities. In those times, a person of African descent was counted as only three-fifths of a person.

The Holocaust was one of the worst horrors in human history. Between 1941 and 1945 across Europe, the Nazi party, under the leadership of Adolf Hitler, systematically murdered over six million Jews. According to the Holocaust Encyclopedia, "In his speeches and writings, Hitler spread his beliefs in *racial* 'purity' and in the *superiority* of the 'Germanic *race*'—what he called an Aryan 'master *race*.'"

The Bible contains references about racism in many different Scriptures. During the first century, it was common to assign different social statuses to people based on their ethnicities. The Bible refers to non-Jews as "foreigners" or "gentiles." As such, foreigners, women, and children were generally regarded as property and owned by the male heads of households and local rulers. Although this system was part of the social order back then, it wasn't right. No human should own or rule over another. The Bible clearly indicates that we should love everyone equally, as God does. Paul writes in Gal. 3:28, *"There is neither Jew nor Greek, there is neither slave nor free, there is neither male nor female; for you are all one in Christ Jesus."* Paul further reveals that there is no more separation because of race or any other difference because in Christ all are one.

Moses wrote, "For the Lord your God is God of gods and Lord of lords, the great God, mighty and awesome, who shows no partiality nor takes a bribe. He administers justice for the fatherless and the widow, and loves the stranger, giving him food and clothing. Therefore love the stranger, for you were strangers in the land of Egypt" (Deut. 10:17–19).

In Acts, we read, "Then Peter opened his mouth and said: 'In truth I perceive that God shows no partiality. But in every nation whoever fears Him and works righteousness is accepted by Him'" (10:34–35).

There are several other Scriptures that echo this same sentiment.

Avoid Faith-Based Pride

Perhaps the priest and the Levite avoided the man because they were part of the religious order of the day, and the man was not. Sadly, faith-based pride is a problem within many religions, including Christianity. Pride has often been a key factor for religions and denominations to be established and even for various splits. Pride is often the cause of upheaval in families and marriages, where one mate forces the other to adopt his or her faith as a condition of marriage.

Faith-based pride can be traced back to Lucifer. Remember that he was bold enough to challenge the system of Heaven!

As hard as it is to face, some Christians look down on non-Christians. It's as though Christians did something more than simply accept God's free-grace gift of salvation! One horrific example of this type of pride was the holy wars known as the Crusades. For almost two hundred years (1095–1291), Christian Crusaders attempted to capture the sacred places in the Holy Land away from the Muslims who lived there. It is estimated that 1.7 million people died during these wars.

In the Bible, the Jewish nation descended from Abraham. They traced their lineage through the Twelve Tribes of Israel and were God's *chosen* people (Deut. 7). Gentiles were everyone else. Jews obeyed the Mosaic law and had specific customs. There were major cultural differences between what Jews and Gentiles ate, how they dressed, how they washed, how they worshipped, and what their art, academics, language, and social customs were like. However, Jesus came to break down the wall between Jews and Gentiles.

One of the most fascinating aspects of this Good Samaritan story is the reference to both religious men passing by on "the other side." Notice that we find these same words in Mark 4:35 and Luke 8:22, when Jesus tells the disciples, "Let's go to the other side." In these texts, Jesus instructs the disciples to come with Him across the Sea of Galilee to go to the land of the Gentiles.

Jesus's instructions to venture into this Gentile land must have been a very puzzling action to the disciples, especially since He originally stated that He had come to reach the "lost sheep of Israel"(Matt. 15:24). However, it was necessary for Jesus to expand the scope of His ministry to fulfill His mission: *"For God did not send His Son into the world to condemn the world, but that the world through Him might be saved"* (John 3:17).

There are several instances of Jesus's demonstration of love for "non-Jews." In Mark 5:8, He healed the demoniac man and then told him to be a witness to others. In Matt. 15:28, Jesus healed the Gentile woman whose daughter was sick. And in John 4, He spoke to the Samaritan woman at the well, which was the longest one-on-one dialogue between Jesus and any person in the Bible! In all three accounts, these Gentiles put their faith in the one, true God and became witnesses to the world.

Going to "the other side" is the act of love that shows the world Jesus!

Avoid "Saving Face" Pride

The concept of "saving face" or "losing face" is an ideal that originated in the 1800s among Asian cultures. To "save face" meant to avoid public humiliation or embarrassment and to maintain dignity or preserve one's reputation.

Would the priest have become "ceremonially unclean" by helping the wounded man? Would the Levite have tarnished his reputation by associating himself with this "common" man?

For many people, even Christians, avoiding embarrassing situations means avoiding being associated with people of a certain class. Many times, we are so busy climbing up the ladder that we step over people who truly need us. A well-known saying declares, "The people you stepped over on the way up are the same people you're going to meet on the way back down!" The Golden Rule found in Matt. 7:12 and Luke 6:31 is summarized, "Do unto others as you would have them do unto you."

A person's current situation doesn't dictate their future. When people you know are in a season of "going through," do you run to help, or do you run away?

As a Christian, you shouldn't be so concerned about your status that you disassociate yourself from people when they make a mistake or have a misstep/fall or are out of favor for whatever reason. Jesus commands us, *"Love your neighbor as yourself "* (Mark 12:31). This means, show love and kindness to everyone regardless of their race, creed, color, status, or situation!

As you meditate on this chapter, please listen to:

"ALPHA & OMEGA"

Chapter Five

WORSHIPPERS MUST BE COMPASSIONATE

But a certain Samaritan, as he journeyed, came where he was. And when he saw him, he had compassion. (Luke 10:33)

All People Matter

In the aftermath of the May 2020 George Floyd killing by a white police officer, we saw the world jump to its feet and take to the streets. The marches and messages caused a tidal wave in favor of the movement and mantra Black Lives Matter. Ironically, the Black Lives Matter movement had begun back in 2013, but it took seven long years and a string of violent acts by police for the message to take hold and begin to resonate with the masses across the globe.

It became clear that those in control of the American systems of power, especially regarding policing, had become so absorbed with procedures, policies, prosperity, prisons, and politics that they had forgotten about the people! The truth is, people matter to God more than anything!

In this parable, Jesus shows us how two men, both heavily involved in the religious systems of the day and both considered good by cultural standards, had *missed* God. As a worshipper, you must be more than passionate, you must be compassionate. Most people are passionate about the things that matter to them, and while this is admirable, it is incomplete. The white police officer that killed George Floyd was passionate about doing his job, but he lacked compassion for the man whom he had sworn to serve and protect.

My warning and plea to all worshippers right now as you read this book is, "Don't miss God!" No matter what position of leadership you occupy or how gifted you are, you must remember to move beyond passion to compassion. Don't be so wrapped up in yourself that you neglect the fact that *people* matter.

Paul writes these words of warning to Timothy, his son in the Gospel: "But know this, that in the last days perilous times will come: For men will be lovers of themselves, lovers of money, boasters, proud, blasphemers, disobedient to parents, unthankful, unholy, unloving, unforgiving, slanderers, without self-control, brutal, despisers of good, traitors, headstrong, haughty, lovers of pleasure rather than lovers of God, having a form of godliness but denying its power. And from such people turn away!" (2 Timothy 3:1–5).

As difficult as it is to hear these harsh words, it's even more challenging to acknowledge that these negative characteristics are found among many believers. We must guard against selfishness and lack of self- control.

First, take honest inventory of your own life. Are you more concerned with *getting*, rather than *giving?* Are you more interested in how things benefit you, rather than how you can be a benefit to others? Are you unwilling to sacrifice your "comfort zone collection" of thoughts, words, and actions? Are you unwilling to forgive your enemies and bless them?

Overcoming the Past Matters

In this parable, Jesus tells us that the man who offered help was a Samaritan. This is extremely significant. The relationship between Samaritans and Jews was one of historic and vehement hatred. They were like the Bloods and the Crips, only worse, because the discord had lasted much longer and ran much deeper.

As far back as 722 BC, there were incidents between Samaritans and Jews that turned them against each other, with various acts done to devastate the other. The Jews considered the Samaritans"half-breeds" and routinely called them "dogs" and other insulting names. By the time Jesus spoke this parable there were centuries of hostility between the two nations.

In American society, as we have witnessed the mistreatment of many African Americans who over the past four-hundred-plus years have been enslaved, beaten, lynched, and imprisoned and now are being gunned down by law enforcement, it's difficult to put the past behind us and move forward. However, there's no room for racial hatred, bigotry, prejudice, or sexism in worship! No matter what has happened in the past, the blood of Jesus still covers, redeems, and renews.

> ***So why did Jesus choose to purposely use a Samaritan in His story? It was to show that the historic biases that we have toward race must be healed because they are unacceptable to God.***

Mind over Matter

Years ago, I was on active duty, stationed at Fort Belvoir, VA. My platoon had two accountability formations each day at 6:00 a.m. and 4:00 p.m. These were mandatory, "no excuses" meetings, despite weather or any other conditions, activities, or concerns. One frigid winter afternoon, I decided to challenge my platoon sergeant regarding the 4:00 p.m. formation. That day, the temperature was only 12 degrees.

"Sergeant," I asked. "Are we going to actually stand outside in that cold weather?" He replied, without hesitation, "We most certainly are! Why wouldn't we?" "The weather!" I responded. "It's freezing out there!" As if he didn't already know.

He looked me squarely in my eyes and coldly responded, "As soldiers, we have to endure the elements. It's 'mind over matter.'"

That was it. "Mind over matter." In those few words, he reminded me that the mind is powerful enough to rise above any physical or emotional situation and operate on a higher level in order to complete every assignment.

What if war broke out in the winter? Would it be acceptable for soldiers to refuse to fight because of the outside temperature? *Absolutely not!*

The same holds true for worshippers. Whether you're in a frontline position of leadership or just one of the background singers, you must always understand the need to look beyond your personal concerns and pursue the presence and purpose of God. Even in the midst of the emotional battles of hurt, pain, disappointment, betrayal, or the loss of loved ones, you must fight through your emotions in order to be effective in your ministry to others.

As a worshipper, you must operate in two realms: *natural and spiritual.* In the book of Revelation, John was physically on the island of Patmos, which was a dreadful place; but he was transported to a spiritual realm where Jesus gave him a glorious vision. This is a powerful example of how we must function in the natural, or earthly, realm but maintain supernatural vision, even in times of stress and challenge. When we keep our "spiritual eyes and ears" in sync with God's vision, we can operate successfully in our God-ordained assignment. This is both the challenge and the blessing of the worshipper! The exciting thing is, God promises to continually provide the spiritual strength necessary to complete His assignment, even though it is inevitable that we will face challenges, both physically and emotionally.

The Matter of Godly Compassion

Over the past twenty-five years or so, media has largely been responsible for systematically desensitizing society. Profanity, nudity, and violence are commonplace on the web, in video games, movies, and television shows. It's to the point that many children are learning more from what they see on the Internet, at movies, and on television than from any classroom teacher, parent, or spiritual mentor. Not only are they learning more, they are learning it at extremely early ages.

As a result, we are seeing troubling behavioral patterns emerge among many young people. There is an overt predisposition to violence accompanied by a lack of empathy and sympathy.

Compassion is defined as "suffering with another" (greatergood.berkeley.edu). It means to literally "feel" the pain of another and respond to it. It's the opposite of what the Bible refers to as a "hard heart."

Worshippers must be compassionate!

Jesus had compassion for people. He commanded, "But love your enemies, do good, and lend, hoping for nothing in return; and your reward will be great, and you will be sons of the Most High. For He is kind to the unthankful and evil. Therefore be merciful, just as your Father also is merciful" (Luke 6:35–36).

There are many biblical examples where Jesus demonstrated compassion. He healed the sick, raised the dead, opened blinded eyes, and fed the multitudes. The Bible tells us that most of the time it was because His heart was "moved to compassion."

It's essential to realize that Jesus not only *felt* the suffering of others, he *took action.* Many times we can feel the burden, pain, and suffering that others are experiencing but fail to take action. Compassion puts love into action.

The Bible says that the Samaritan man first felt and then acted. If you see someone suffering, whether emotionally, physically, or spiritually, your kind words and prayers are great but they need to be accompanied with action. Remember, love is a verb.

LET'S PRAY!

Father, please continue to draw me close to You and strengthen my heart so that I can grow in Your love. I need the continued healing and restoration that only You can give. God, please fix my heart and destroy the cycles of hurt, rejection, and pain that I have experienced as I have endeavored to do Your will.

I pray that nothing and no one will block the flow ofYour anointing in my life and that each day I will become stronger in my fellowship with You and with others. As I cultivate my relationship with You, I humbly ask You to dispatch ministering angels to whisper Your words into my ear gates.

Lord, regulate my mind and cause me to bring every thought into captivity to Your will and make my thoughts obedient to Your word. Father, as I worship, I continually stir up the gift that You put inside me. Please let Your power rise up big on the inside of me so that Your name will be glorified on the outside of me.

I decree and declare that I am healed, whole, and complete.

In Jesus's Name, Amen.

SECTION THREE

Love Builds Others Up

Chapter Six

FIRST, STOP THE BLEEDING!

"So he went to him and bandaged his wounds, pouring on oil and wine; and he set him on his own animal, brought him to an inn, and took care of him."
(Luke 10:34)

As believers, we must always be prepared to minister to those who are suffering. Whether a person's injuries are physical, emotional, or spiritual, we are called to meet needs, regardless of a person's past or current status.

Sometimes you will encounter people who have been beaten down by the challenges of life. They have been stripped of their joy, they have no peace, and they've lost sight of God.

Often, these people are gushing with negative thoughts, words, and actions. They don't have any respect for themselves or anyone else. They are half dead and have given up on their dreams and moved off the path of Godly purpose. When you encounter this type of person, the challenge to you is whether to move on with your life (pass by on the other side) or stop and minister to the needs of that half-dead individual.

The awesome thing about this parable is that it can be applied to any specific individual that you may encounter in a terrible situation, or it can symbolize in general the sin-dark world in which we live, where so many people are physically alive but emotionally and spiritually *half dead.*

Jesus tells us exactly what to do. *First, you must stoop down and stop the bleeding.* You must humble yourself and realize that it is only by God's grace that you have been saved from a similar (or worse) predicament, and only because of God's mercy that you have not been consumed. If it had not been for God's unmerited favor and amazing grace that was poured out on your life through the shed blood of Jesus Christ, you could very well be lying there in the same ditch.

In his book *Humility: The Journey Toward Holiness,* author and theologian Andrew Murray wrote, "Humility is the displacement of self by the enthronement of God." C. S. Lewis stated, "Humility is not thinking less of yourself; it's thinking of yourself less." I Peter 5:6 says, *"Therefore humble yourselves under the mighty hand of God, that He may exalt you in due time."*

Humility is the opposite of pride, and it should be the hallmark of every believer. Humility can be defined as "a critical and continuous emphasis of godliness" (Christianity.com). This definition moves beyond mental, physical, and emotional subservience and indicates a higher level of abiding or dwelling in the place of God's purpose and presence.

Abiding in His presence is essential in order to cultivate true humility.

Second, Address the Problem

The Samaritan didn't start praying and speaking in tongues over the wounded man, he stooped down and began to pour olive oil and wine into the man's wounds. Sometimes we fail to address problems that are raging in our own lives or in the lives of others in a practical way.

When you abide "in" God, you receive a vertical download of His love. It is only then that you are able to show true unconditional love to others that builds them up and never destroys.

An old saying affirms, "Don't be so spiritually minded that you're no earthly good!"

The Samaritan addressed the issue in a literal way.

Oil was a cleansing agent. It was an ointment that was applied to help soothe the man's injuries. It also represented the presence of the Spirit of God as well as God's mercy (Ps. 52:8). Oil was also used ceremonially to consecrate and make holy. The Samaritan poured wine to disinfect the wound. In the days of the Bible, wine was much stronger and had the ability to kill bacteria. Wine also represented the cleansing power of the blood of Jesus. In a literal sense, the Samaritan demonstrated the fact that we must operate in two realms, natural and supernatural.

When a person is half dead, he or she certainly needs the presence and power of God for renewal and healing, but the person may also need counseling or medical attention. Just as the Samaritan offered first aid to this wounded man, we must offer practical solutions to the problems in us and around us.

He Bandaged Him Up

Here is where the parable really takes on momentum. In biblical times, olive oil and wine were common commodities in Israel. There were different "grades" of these items, but almost all people had a supply of both. The Samaritan likely was carrying olive oil and wine with him on his journey. However, when it came to bandages, it is unlikely that he had any with him. So where did the bandages come from?

He probably had to take some of his own good clothing and tear it up to use as bandages to wrap around the wounded man. This meant sacrificing garments that would never again be usable.

When we consider the agape love the Samaritan exhibited in sacrificing his personal clothing as bandages for the injured man, we must consider that he did not look at his sacrifice as a loss but as a gain.

This reminds me of my grandmother's explanation of salvation. When I was around twelve, she said to me, "Imagine getting a beautifully wrapped gift in the mail and there was no occasion. Inside this package there was something very special. When you opened it, to your amazement you discovered that the giver was someone you'd been unkind to and had even avoided. That's the example of the Father's grace. There was no special occasion, but He sent His Son Jesus Christ to earth because He was determined to save and redeem us from the curse and penalty of sin."

I'm glad that God looked past the fact that each one of us has, at one time or another, ignored and rebelled against Him. Nevertheless, He extended, and continues to extend, His grace when we do not deserve it, could never earn it, and can never repay it. The Samaritan had mercy on the wounded man with no thought of being repaid.

The man was beaten and bloody but the Samaritan didn't hesitate to rip up his good clothes.

In Psalm 147:1–3, David wrote, "Praise the Lord! For *it is* good to sing praises to our God; For *it is* pleasant, *and* praise is beautiful. The Lord builds up Jerusalem; He gathers together the outcasts of Israel. He heals the brokenhearted and binds up their wounds."

In this portion of the parable especially, we see a foretaste of Jesus's own sacrifice that would heal the sin-sick, restore the broken, and revive the half dead. Jesus would pay a debt that He did not owe.

As you meditate on this chapter, please listen to:

"THE LORD IS HERE"

Chapter Seven

LOVE LIFTS AND PROTECTS

So he went to him and bandaged his wounds, pouring on oil and wine; and he set him on his own animal, brought him to an inn, and took care of him. (Luke 10:34)

An old hymn of the church, "Love Lifted Me," declares:

"I was sinking deep in sin,

Far from the peaceful shore,

Very deeply stained within,

Sinking to rise no more;

But the Master of the sea

Heard my despairing cry,

From the waters lifted me,

Now safe am I."

The idea that the Samaritan lifted this man indicates the man was unable to lift himself. There are times in all of our lives when we are unable to lift ourselves out of various situations.

David wrote in Psalm 40:1–3, "I waited patiently for the Lord; And He inclined to me, And heard my cry. He also brought me up out of a horrible pit, Out of the miry clay, And set my feet upon a rock, And established my steps. He has put a new song in my mouth—Praise to our God; Many will see it and fear, And will trust in the Lord."

David was in a horrible situation and couldn't get himself out of it; he needed God to intervene. Whether you are in a spiritual, physical, or emotional pit or someone you know is in a terrible predicament, my counsel to you is to look up and allow God to lift you up or go and lift up someone else.

Both the hymnist and psalmist speak to situations of helplessness and hopelessness. The writer of the hymn tells of a person who was sinking, stained and unsecured. The psalmist tells of a pit, not just a low place but a place that was horrible and miry. The idea of the "miry clay" is a dark, foul-smelling pit where stagnant water and other decaying debris has collected. It is slimy and slippery in this miry pit, and you can't get your footing to climb up and out. It is this type of pit, whether emotional or spiritual, that people often experience and, left by themselves, have no way of getting out of.

Love Responds to Crisis

The Samaritan heard the man's cries of despair and responded.

When we consider this wounded man, bloodied and half dead, lying on the roadside, we can imagine that he probably didn't have a lot of strength by the time the Samaritan showed up. Remember, the priest and the Levite had already passed him by. Perhaps when they came by he was able to cry out more loudly. But by the time the Samaritan came by the man was only able to moan and groan.

Sometimes we think that God doesn't hear us or that He only hears us when we are loud, but Isaiah reminds us, *"Behold, the Lord's hand is not shortened, That it cannot save; Nor His ear heavy, That it cannot hear"* (Isaiah 59:1).

> ***Whether you cry out or moan doesn't matter. God is always listening and always ready to respond to the cry of His children. He sees, He hears, and He cares.***

Whether you cry out or moan doesn't matter. God is always listening and always ready to respond to the cry of His children. He sees, He hears, and He cares.

Love always has an attentive ear and is ready to respond in times of crisis.

Love Provides a Safe Place

The Samaritan took him to an inn, a place of safety. In this place, the Samaritan could focus on restoring the wounded man.

The safe place is sometimes a secret place, but it is always a necessary place. In this place, a person is insulated and isolated from infectious, life-threatening elements. There are no distractions, dangers, or enemies in the safe place.

The safe place is like a luxury hotel where there's warmth and security, but most importantly where distractions are eliminated.

Have you ever been to a cheap hotel? Without being condescending, there are some hotels where you drive up and there are no elevators; you must lug your bags up the metal staircase, and once you get into your room, you can hear whatever's going on next door through the thin walls. The bathroom is small, the shower is dingy, and you feel unprotected and insecure.

On the other hand, one of my favorite hotels offers valet parking, attentive front desk clerks, and efficient processing of room requests. The bellhops quickly take the luggage and place it on a clean cart and escort you to the elevator as they point out the location and hours of the restaurant and various other amenities. When you get in the elevator to go to your room, as a security measure you have to insert your key card to access your floor. The maid has already been in your room to make sure that all the fixtures and bedding are neat, clean, and fresh. There is a card on your bed with the name and phone number of the housekeeping staff member, to ensure that things are sanitary and disinfected. The bathroom is bright and shiny, and the towels and bathrobes are thick and lush. There is a twenty-four-hour doorman and a security guard to make sure that all guests and premises are protected at all times. When you're at a place like this, you can work, rest, eat, or exercise with a superior level of comfort. It's like the song "Leaning on Jesus" says: "Safe and secure from all alarms."

In a safe place, you can heal from wounds and recover from pain. Although the wounded man was left half dead, the Samaritan carried him to a place of refuge and safety!

As a worshipper, you may have become mentally, physically, and spiritually wounded. If so, just cry out to God and allow Him to transport you to a safe place—away from the distractions, dangers, and enemies of your soul! In the safe place you can find healing.

Please don't continue to try to go forward in your assignment if you need to retreat to a safe place! Pain can make you prideful. In fact, you can get so prideful that you fail to heed the warning signs, and you refuse to stop and retreat to a safe place. This mindset can be very harmful to your assignment. It's like being infected with poisonous venom and refusing the antidote. A wounded worshipper will bleed on people who didn't cut him (or her)!

If you've been wounded, take time now to get to a safe place and rid yourself of the poison of your past before going back in front of the people. In my experience, I've seen wounded worshippers or worship leaders attempt to transfer to a new setting without taking time to receive healing. This is a recipe that perpetuates cycles of disaster. First, go and be restored in a safe place so that ultimately you will be able to function in your assignment at full capacity.

As you meditate on this chapter, please listen to:

"YOUR VOICE"

Chapter Eight

THE IMPORTANCE OF THE HEALING PROCESS

On the next day, when he departed, he took out two denarii, gave them to the innkeeper, and said to him, "Take care of him; and whatever more you spend, when I come again, I will repay you."(Luke 10:35)

What's in your heart abundantly will come out of your mouth eventually. In this chapter, I want to underscore the connection between love and healing. You may have a genuine love for God, and your worship may be authentic; however, without healing and restoration, any hurt, pain, rejection, betrayal, or other venomous poison inside your heart will spew out as you attempt to worship. If you don't heal, your pain will become poisonous and your worship will be contaminated.

It's not what or who is outside you that's the problem—it's what's inside you.

I'm reminded of the biblical account in Mark 7:1–23, when Jesus and His disciples were eating together, and the Pharisees made a big deal about the fact that the disciples were eating without ceremonially washing their hands. Back then, the ceremonial washing of hands was a religious tradition more than an act of cleanliness.

But Jesus responded to the Pharisees, "There is nothing that enters a man from outside which can defile him; but the things which come out of him, those are the things that defile a man" (Mark 7:15).

Healing doesn't happen overnight.

One thing that we see in the parable is that the Samaritan stayed with the man through the night until the next morning. The Samaritan had already been delayed on his journey, had used his own oil and wine, had torn up his clothes, and had walked while the wounded man rode on his donkey. He then checked into the inn and paid for everything. Beyond the sacrifice of his belongings and finances, the Samaritan chose to sacrifice his sleep and comfort! No doubt that throughout the night he had to redress the man's wounds and re-bandage him. It was a sleepless night in a room with a stranger! But he didn't stop there. Jesus tells us the Samaritan made long-term arrangements for the wounded man.

In Matthew 6:21, we find the words of Jesus: *"For where your treasure is, there your heart will be also."* What was the worth of the two denarii that the Samaritan provided for the man's care? According to the American Bible Society (americanbible.org), there are two possibilities: The first was that the coins would take care of the man for two weeks; the second analysis states that the money would provide care for two months!

> ***When we think about the standards and normal patterns of today's society, most people, even Christians, are more like the priest and the Levite than the Samaritan.***

We are far too busy to be bothered with the concerns of others! We seriously don't want to be inconvenienced, and unless we feel like something or someone can benefit us, we rarely want to become involved. We talk about Kingdom and unity, but many times we operate selfishly. This is bad enough when it comes to time and talent, but when it comes to our money (treasure), the Bible is clear on the mandate to tithe and give offerings, but what about giving money to help others in difficult situations?

Our assignment as worshippers is to build God's Kingdom on earth. Paul wrote, *"For as the body is one and has many members, but all the members of that one body, being many, are one body, so also is Christ"* (I Corinthian 12:12). Society is made up of people of different backgrounds, colors, and beliefs, but all are God's children. As individuals, we are assigned to build others up and when necessary lift each other up and be part of the healing process! Sometimes, that means financial provision.

The healing process is similar to the process of building a house. When I built my house, it was so nerve racking! The contractors were constantly calling, asking me things like, "What type of grout do you want? What type of countertops? What kind of flooring?" And all sorts of other details. When you're in the process of building somebody up, you've got to take time to deal with the details of their situation to make sure all bases are covered. We have to be specific in our support, whether it's prayers and intercession or money and other resources. Our responsibility is to respond to those in need and assist in the healing process.

Healing Is More than Serving, It's Caring

As the wounded man lay bleeding on the roadside, the trauma he had experienced at the hands of the robbers had left him half dead. But there was another important observation to be made regarding this man. The Samaritan recognized it; this man was also *half alive!*

No matter how bad a situation is or how low a person has gotten, it is the charge of every worshipper to see others as God sees them. After taking the man to a place of safety and watching over him during the night, the Samaritan knew that the restoration process would require on-going care and attention. He entrusted the man to the innkeeper for the process of healing to take place, and he indicated that he'd return and pay the expenses for the man's recovery process.

How many of us would show that level of care and concern for a complete stranger? Do you really care for people? Or is your love conditional and situational? God calls us to foster people's total restoration!

Many worshippers don't believe that total healing and restoration is possible! But if you don't believe it then you don't believe the Bible. Matthew reported, "And Jesus went about all Galilee, teaching in their synagogues, preaching the gospel of the kingdom, and healing all kinds of sickness and all kinds of disease among the people. Then His fame went throughout all Syria; and they brought to Him all sick people who were afflicted with various diseases and torments, and those who were demon-possessed, epileptics, and paralytics; and He healed them" (Matthew 4:23–24).

When you are assigned to oversee others, you must see past their temporary circumstances and see them to the goal of total healing. One thing that happened with the 2020 COVID-19 pandemic was that many United States governors opened their states up as a measure to restart the economy before the number of cases in their states declined significantly. In many cases, many more lives were lost because it was too soon to go back to "business as usual" when the virus was still spiraling out of control and there was no vaccine.

Caring means that you must get involved with the management of the healing process. This often requires time and resources, but true leaders who have a heart for people will expend the time and financial resources needed to see the healing process all the way through to completion.

Great leaders understand that they are blessed to be a blessing.

Generosity

One of the hallmarks of great leaders is generosity. Jesus said, "Give, and it will be given to you: good measure, pressed down, shaken together, and running over will be put into your bosom. For with the same measure that you use, it will be measured back to you" (Luke 6:38).

Pastors aren't the only leaders to which this Scripture applies. As worshippers, we are included in this mandate to give. Many times, as worship leaders, we must rise up early, be among the first to arrive at church and among the last to leave. We must set the atmosphere and the standard from the house of worship to our homes! This means that we can't look at our service of time and talent as our total "gift." Many worship leaders feel as though they don't have to tithe and give offerings because they give so much of their service to their local ministry. God loves a cheerful, extravagant giver! When you stop or hold back your seed, you limit your harvest.

Pouring out from your substance is about everything you have—your time, talent, and money! If we are cheerful givers, we will be likewise rewarded; the opposite is also true. The only way you can rise to this level is that your heart is filled with the love of God, which again demands that you abide in His presence. There is no way that you can be a cheerful giver without loving God and loving what God loves.

Wisdom and Discernment

In order to be a good steward, the Samaritan had to hear from God. How ironic it was that the religious men, the priest and the Levite, passed by the wounded man, and the despised Samaritan was the one that showed Godly love, generosity, wisdom, and discernment.

Wisdom is "the capacity to appropriate knowledge" and discernment is "the ability to exercise good judgment." Without wisdom, knowledge can be misguided, and without discernment you can be involved in "good" work but miss out on "God" work. A simpler description is that wisdom guides you in how to handle a situation and discernment guides you in what situations to handle and what situations to leave alone.

God establishes leaders from the heart first, not the head. Although you may be gifted and intellectually capable of charting the course for your ministry, your choir, or your group, your leadership is not a license to rule over others. Without wisdom and discernment you may function in the assignment, but you will miss critical details of the assignment. The proper stewardship of your time, talent, and treasure demands wisdom and discernment.

As you meditate on this chapter, please listen to:

"FATHER I WORSHIP YOU"

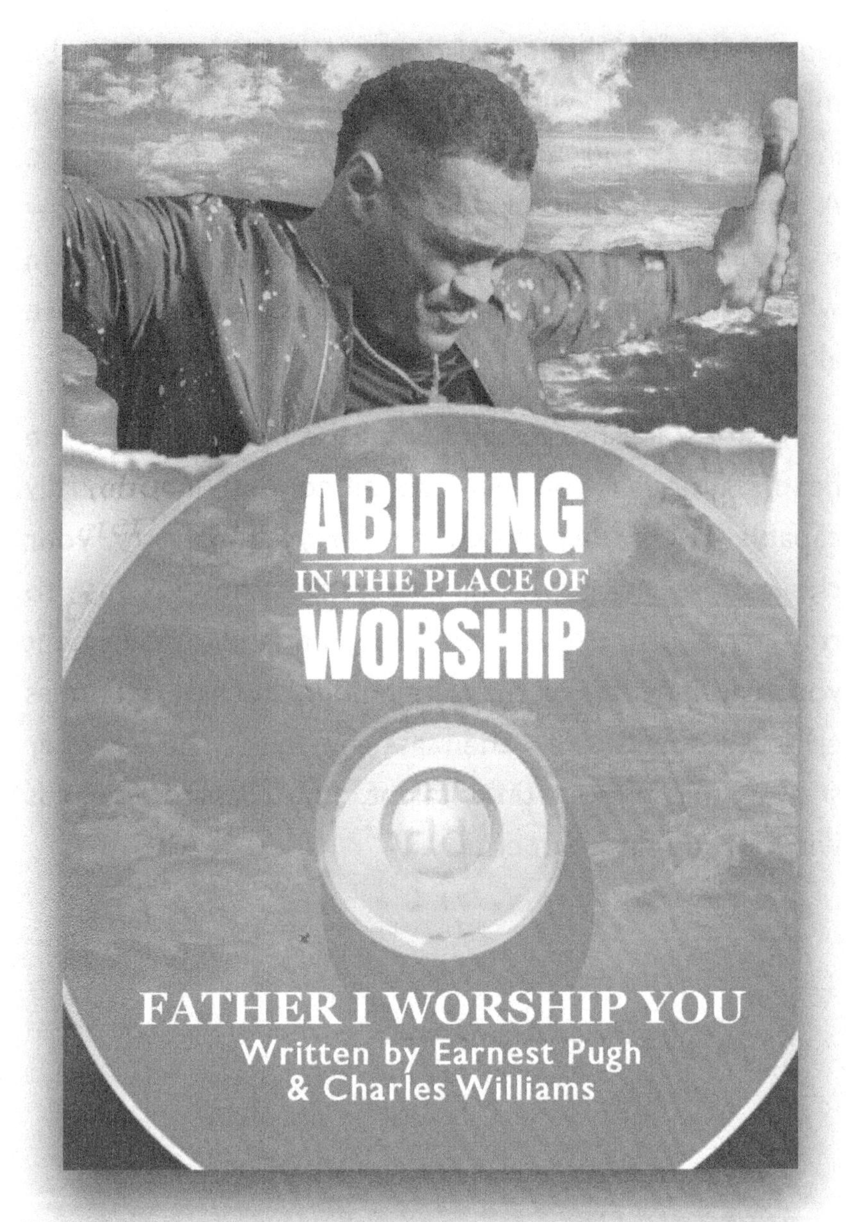

Chapter Nine

UNTIL I RETURN

Throughout this book, I have challenged worshippers and especially worship leaders to exhibit God's love to others, regardless of class, race, creed, education, or background. However, in the post-George Floyd world we live in (not to mention the hundreds, maybe even thousands of names that historically have suffered similarly horrific experiences), things are different, and we must respond to the crisis of today.

Racism, Post-George Floyd

Racism and the resulting brutal treatment are not new phenomena. In fact, this is a problem that has evolved for centuries; so how shall we handle this?

I often say, "When you see what God sees, you'll say what God says." God created us all equal, and even though God sees (and enjoys) the diversity of color, He loves each color He made and desires that we live in harmony and love with unity. This challenges us to see each other as God sees us.

I want to address the racial divide from a very personal place.

I grew up in Memphis,TN. When I was in the ninth grade, getting ready to go to high school, I had two cousins who were both dating Caucasian young ladies. We all went to school together.

I was walking to the bus one day with some other friends who lived near me, and I saw something that traumatized me.

I saw my two cousins hanging from trees. They had been lynched; but not only that, they'd been castrated. A note had been left near the trees with the words, "White girls are off limits to y'all."

Instantly, I felt unimaginable pain and hurt in my heart. From that day, I struggled with bitterness and hatred towards the white men who did that. Those boys they killed were my relatives that should be here today, but because these men didn't value my cousin's lives, they did a horrible deed and were never caught or prosecuted.

Even with my high school prom, we had to literally have a protest march so that we could combine blacks and whites at the same prom. Many of the white parents didn't feel we were worthy to go to the same prom as the Caucasian kids.

It took me a long time to get past those things. I had to continually pray so that I wouldn't internalize the anger or retaliate and react. Thankfully, when I joined the military out of high school, I found that they were big on race relations. That helped to balance me and expand my mind regarding other races. The other helpful thing was that I studied the Scriptures to really see how I was supposed to deal with the racial divisions in my personal experience and in the world at large.

It wasn't easy. It was a process. My heart was wounded, and I needed healing! I went through counseling because I had a lot of anger issues and 90 percent of them centered around racism. I had to learn how to forgive. My counselor would tell me, "Rather than pluck the fruit, we're going to deal with the root, and the root of the matter is that you're angry, bitter, and frustrated. First, let's deal with forgiveness. Can you forgive them?"

So I had to say this confession: "I forgive all Caucasians. I erase the incidents out of my mind that they've done to make me hate them. I'm going to love them with the same love that Christ loved the church."

Sometimes, I would say the confession, but I'd still see my dead cousins' bodies flash in front of my face, and when I would see a white person I'd feel anger rise up in my heart. I would think about every past generation of that person's family and imagine how they must have devalued the lives of black people. It took time to heal my mind and spirit of those wounds, but I was determined to pull down that mindset of hatred and replace it with love.

As I've been saying throughout this book, love is an action word, it's a verb. I purposely began to go out of my way to show love to Caucasians. I felt like, "If they're full of hell and I'm full of love, then I'll love the hell out of them." That became my mindset.

I also joined a non-denominational church that was 40 percent Black, about 20 percent Caucasian, and the rest Hispanic. As a worship leader, I went after Caucasians to be on my team. I couldn't preach or sing about a Black Jesus; I learned to just preach the love of God.

Hatred is not about personality, it's about a principality.

You can't fully worship God with a heart that contains things that are contrary to His nature. When I learned how to forgive, it really let me see people for who they really were. I know that worship changes atmospheres, and because I gained victory over the atmosphere in my own heart, I became empowered to shift atmospheres through my worship.

I would tell my Caucasian friends to educate themselves and just listen to a little bit of what the Black experience has been. As I see what's happening in this post-George Floyd society, I am hopeful and optimistic that this is a season of lasting change for race relations.

Worshippers Must Be Prayer Warriors

The most important thing for worshippers to do is to pray. This is the most effective way to learn God's *heart* on matters. Prayer makes you intimate with God. It doesn't matter who or what comes against you, your intimacy with God will change your heart by making you sensitive to the *voice* of the Holy Spirit. We must learn to pray for our enemies. Jesus said, *"Bless those who curse you, and pray for those who spitefully use you"* (Luke 6:28).

I have some Caucasian friends who used to refer to me as "a colored guy" or "my Black friend." I was insulted, and it really caused me to pray about how to deal with them. I'm very confrontational, but God said, "No, no, no! I don't want you to react, I want you to respond." My resposnse was to speak the word of God over those persons, and I saw transformation in them over a number of years. It was slower than what I felt like it would have been if I had just *laid my hands on them* (not holy hands!), but I saw transformation as a a result of me praying and speaking the word of God over the situation and talking honestly to them about the offense their words brought.

> ***In the midst of so much racism in our country and even in the gospel music industry, God is still able to bring something great out of all of this.***

Our job as worshippers is to put God's word in the atmosphere, and I believe we will eventually see Caucasians and African Americans come together.

I believe we will see pastors and worship leaders and congregations come together. God's house will be a house of prayer for all *ethnos*, which means all ethnicities—people from different backgrounds and with different skin colorations. (Isaiah 56:7)

Nothing happens until we get on one accord! Even when we go back to the day of Pentecost, the Holy Ghost didn't even come in until they got on one accord.

Worship leaders! We must get the atmosphere ready for the Holy Spirit to move and dwell and meet the needs of God's people. It's in our unity that we have power.

LET'S PRAY

Dear Lord,

I come before You, thanking You for a heart of compassion that compels me to encourage, edify, and empower my fellow man. It is my sincere desire to see them as you see them and treat them accordingly.

As I encounter those who have strayed from the path of righteousness, please enable me to be the kind of first responder that allows Your love to prevail in that moment so that I may quickly help restore them to their path of purpose.

Lord Jesus, please allow the spirit of humility to compel me to stoop down with a sense of urgency to render immediate help, aid, and assistance to those who need to be rebuilt and restored to their rightful place in you.

Father, Your Word declares in 3 John 1:2, "Beloved, I pray that you may prosper in all things and be in health, just as your soul prospers." Just as total healing for mankind is Your top priority, I, likewise, make it my priority as You use me for Your service in the Kingdom. And it is so.

In Jesus's Name, Amen.

About the Author

Dr. Earnest L. Pugh has conducted worship seminars, conferences and concerts for over thirty years!

During his tenure as a worship leader, he simultaneously served as a national recording artist, producing twelve CDs. He has been celebrated on three separate occasions by Billboard Magazine as the #1 artist on the Gospel chart.

Dr. Pugh has traveled extensively throughout the United States and internationally. He has ministered in England, Africa, Italy, Europe, Korea and Australia. He is passionate about sharing his wealth of insight regarding the marriage between the pulpit and music pit.

Made in the USA
Middletown, DE
27 June 2022

67708565R00060